HAPPYAGONY

HAPPYAGONY

A COLLECTION OF POEMS

BY MEM FERDA

T

Troubador Publishing Ltd
Unit E2 Airfield Business Park,
Harrison Road, Market Harborough,
Leicestershire. LE16 7UL
Tel: 0116 279 2299
Email: books@troubador.co.uk
Web: www.troubador.co.uk

ISBN 978 1836280 385

British Library Cataloguing in Publication Data.
A catalogue record for this book is available from the British Library.

Printed and bound by CPI Group (UK) Ltd, Croydon, CR0 4YY
Typeset in 13pt Calibri by Troubador Publishing Ltd, Leicester, UK

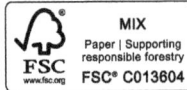

MIX
Paper | Supporting
responsible forestry
FSC
www.fsc.org   FSC® C013604

For Aydın

CONTENTS

SOCIETY

LOVE

GRIEF

ACKNOWLEDGEMENTS

I dedicate this book of poetry to my dearest sister, Aydın, who we tragically lost during my teenage years. Also, to my beloved parents, who were instrumental in encouraging my creative abilities. To my mother, thank you for having me recite poetry from the tender age of five, standing on a footstool at family gatherings. And to my father, thank you for passing on your poetic genius into my DNA.

To my beautiful wife, Rabia, your love has been by far the greatest catalyst for my growth. Thanks to your belief in me, I have reached heights I never thought possible. Your sacrifices have enabled me to pursue and share my passions with the world. Your presence in my life is an incomparable gift.

To the countless souls who have touched my life, in one way or another, thank you. You have shaped me profoundly through our conversations, shared experiences and encounters. To my family and friends – you know who you are – your kindness and encouragement have left an enduring mark on my heart. I am eternally grateful to you all.

With love and gratitude,
Mem

YOUTH

BYGONE REBEL

Remember the bygone years,
set so long now in the past,
where nightclubs were my church.
I worshipped endlessly
through the nights.

Sweltering summer sex
amid beautiful shapely girls,
perfumed bottles and ice
for souls who dared to imbibe.

Drink— and drug-fuelled laughter,
secrets I wish I could deny,
soiled carpets, beer and ash,
battered knuckles, bruised and dry.

My motorbike, agile and fast,
incessantly roaring in a race
with thunderclouds, enchanting
Heaven and Hell to collide.

Oh, the thrill of bygone years,
set so long now in the past.

CHILDHOOD WELL (ANGOLEM)

With cropped hair, barefoot,
in vest and pants, I run
through pale-yellow buildings
and sandy streets of dust
in the scorching afternoon sun.
Ferocious heat beats down
on the weathered village of old
Angolem.

My childhood abode, an almost forgotten land.
Fields of watermelons and orange groves.
I learned early lessons in life,
for here resided some of the wisest,
most philosophical, humblest people on earth.

The village centrepiece was a sandstone water well,
standing solid, stout, and proud,
constructed by my dear, innovative father
during a prolonged drought.
To this day, its presence draws a curious crowd.

With pots and pails, every villager came
to fetch their daily supply of fresh, clean water.
A sense of community and unity
developed around this unassailable well,

where the old and young would gather.
In the sun-kissed summer days
when children relished opportunities to play,
friendships formed and bloomed,
drinking the purest, tastiest water, excavated.

Smiling farmers brought their parched donkeys,
their trusty steeds, to quench their thirst with natural
cold water.
With hungry gulps, the donkeys would drink and rest,
their bodies refreshed for another day's slaughter!

Mesmerised by its depths,
I'd stare for hours into the well,
toss a stone, make a request,
knowing good luck would come.
Sorrowfully, the opposite transpired—
a small Kokoni dog
strayed from his master and fell deep into the abyss.
Efforts made to save the pup failed to prevail.

It was a much-loved pup, doted on by
all the village children.
His owner, the local baker,
was devastated and undone,
for he had adopted the pup for his sick young son,
his muscles wasted with weakness
from a chronic disease—
the drowned pup was his lifeline, not merely for fun.

Tear-filled eyes and heavy hearts gathered
around the well that night.
Mourners drew water and filled pots with flowers.
The air lingered with a scent of despair
as my father announced
the well's closure.
Years have passed, and times have changed,
but the old sandstone well remains—
the water dried-up, swinging buckets packed away,
closed forever on that fateful day.
But from those dusty streets of Angolem,
I'll remember forever the well my father built
with love abiding in my heart.

THE MEERSCHAUM PIPE

His voice quivering with excitement to the very end,
he explained the journey—a trade mission to Cyprus.
They would sail with merchandise in hand:

During their final sea voyage,
in 1866, my great-grandfather
and my grandfather,
the father and son duo,
travelled from
Turkey to Cyprus, onboard
a cargo sailing ship.

During those winter months,
the Mediterranean was
treacherous.
Great-grandfather's health
deteriorated,
body weakened,
spirit remaining adventurous.

The once-strong man
with a heart full of fire
was now fragile and fatigued,
defiant and fighting
for every breath,
despite knowing his life
was soon to be extinguished.

My grandfather's
world shattered,
witnessing his dear father take his
very last breath.
Overwhelmed and shocked,
he quickly took stock,
deftly extracting
a Meerschaum pipe
from his outer pocket.

The urgency was palpable,
as time was
breathing down on him.
He filled the pipe
with his finest tobacco,
lit it,
and set his hat tenderly
atop his father's head,
sitting close beside him.

Every sound was magnified.
The faint scent of saltwater
mingled with the musty
odour of the old pipe,
causing him even more tension.
To draw any notice now
would be fatal.
It would result in my
great-grandfather
being hurled overboard
to the ravenous sharks
and curious sea creatures

that lurked beneath, waiting.
My grandfather protected
the body of his father, until
the voyage's end,
giving the impression
that great-grandfather was quietly
relaxing, while enjoying his favourite tobacco.

My grandfather watched
as time slowly passed,
praying for tomorrow.

The next day,
they arrived
on the shores of Cyprus.
Mourners gathered,
through tears and heavy hearts,
to reminisce about my remarkable
great-grandfather
as they laid him to eternal rest
with the utmost warmth,
respect and kindness.

The waves that lapped the shore did softly whisper,
'Farewell, brave soul; may your journey be gentle
and bright.'

CIRCUMCISION

The rite of passage,
a proud ordeal,
now seems, to me, surreal.
'Look up to the ceiling,
you'll see a mouse, my son.'
—a distraction tactic
to ease a child's mind.

All I saw
was an Ottoman sword,
sharp and strong,
with a warrior's pride.
Now, as I recall,
with dread inside,
its slice through my young flesh.
I thought I had died.

I was placed on a donkey
in my crown and sash,
as hundreds paid homage
and gathered about.
Presents flowed as the
drum and zurna filled the air
in a serenade,
as we continued my masquerade
in our village of Angolem.

My parents looked on,
ever so proudly,
and glowing with elation
at their son becoming a man.
But I couldn't help
my agitation as the bedsheets
brushed my penis:
a burning, torturous pain.

My mother kissed my cheek,
brushing my hair aside
to whisper, 'Maşhallah—'
the same word embroidered
in gold across my sash,
resting on my heart.
'God has willed it,' I said.
'Indeed, he has,' she smiled.

Looking back,
it was a frightful experience,
but one that brings me pride.
My entrance into manhood
was by way of tradition,
marked by the sword
amid an honourable crowd.

CONSEQUENCE

I was startled awake at 2:30 A.M.
by a heinous crime,
a familiar figure in my line of sight!
He hastily handed me a Beretta handgun,
wrapped in cloth, seething as he whispered,
'Hide this,' and I froze.

I knew I wouldn't have been there
if not for his sister so fair,
another consequence of being hooked
on beauty and eloquence.

Despite my fondness for her,
I would vehemently refuse
to be burdened by a life of crime
or stand accused.

Anguished, tormented, and
ignited in the night,
I turned from the gun and
instinctually took flight,
refusing to be an accessory
to something so sinister.

Upon hearing of the evidence
hidden in her basement,
illuminating the horror at first rays of light,
jury members glared,
relatives released tears,
bleeding as they stared.
Retribution justly won
finally banished fears.

But iron bars cannot heal
a violent, warped mind.
Filled-in cracks in concrete walls
cannot disguise
a fate to which we all relate.

He was sentenced
and imprisoned for the strife,
forever for that night.
A life for a life.

THE STATION GRILL

On the corner of Braganza Street
stood a restaurant, oh so neat,
run by my aunt and uncle, dear,
and their two sons, full of cheer.

Inside, you'd hear a symphony of sounds—
shouting, laughter, and family rounds.
In the kitchen, a lively scene,
were delicious dishes, fit for a queen.

At times, it seemed like a family feud,
but then, out came the most scrumptious food,
worth every penny, that's for sure.
I'd scoff spaghetti bolognese with chips galore.

Behind the bar stood Ali— tall,
a master sommelier, charming all.
With his well-mannered talk and friendly smile,
he made every customer feel worthwhile.

Walls adorned with amber lampshades,
complete with gold fringe tassels to match,
cast a warm glow across the tables,
adding to the ambiance, so lush.

There was red velvet wallpaper I often liked to touch,
and matching patterned carpets—
intricate, rich, and plush.

In this hidden corner, we drank,
and shared stories, hopes and doubts.
The world outside seemed so loud,
yet Station Grill was cosy, devout,
our sanctuary away from the crowds.

If you ever find yourself on the corner
of Braganza Street, you might want to step inside,
to join this familial little retreat.

But sadly, the restaurant is no more,
replaced by ultra-modern, expensive flats.
I can't help but feel a sense of pain
for the memories that remain
on the corner on Braganza Street.

OH DONER

Oh, how I adore a doner kebab,
at any time, on any occasion,
rotating on a vertical spit,
so tempting, so tantalising.

The aroma whisks me to Turkey,
the land of its origin,
where "doner" means "turning".
Spinning your taste buds
like a whirling dervish.

Nestled inside a warm pitta,
the juicy carvings are succulently hot.
Tender shreds of lamb mince
are both delicate and soft and yet
robust, spicy, and crisp!

Oh my God! I begin to salivate,
anxious for my first bite
as the chap smiling behind the counter asks,
'Would you like chilli sauce and salad with that?'
'Of course, mate!'

The first bite brings euphoric bliss.
Flavours dance on my tongue, divine.

No need for fancy plates and forks,
these hands will do just fine.
I savour every morsel, every single bite,
as chilli sauce and oil trickle down my
neck at once.

Lettuce, cabbage, onion, and tomatoes
add to the orchestra within the mouth.
The chilli sauce has a mind of its own,
at times, mild and gentle,
with a subtle hint of spice,
or fully grown, in a fiery blaze,
will knock you the spark out!

2:00 A.M. is the best time to devour a doner kebab,
after clubbing and intoxicating, trying for a date—
it's both your friend and your pound of flesh
for the night,
when you had no other luck in sight!

Washing it down with a cold Fanta,
I really could do with another!
From Istanbul to Berlin, New York to Dubai,
this culinary sensation has spread far and wide.
Oh, how I adore a doner.

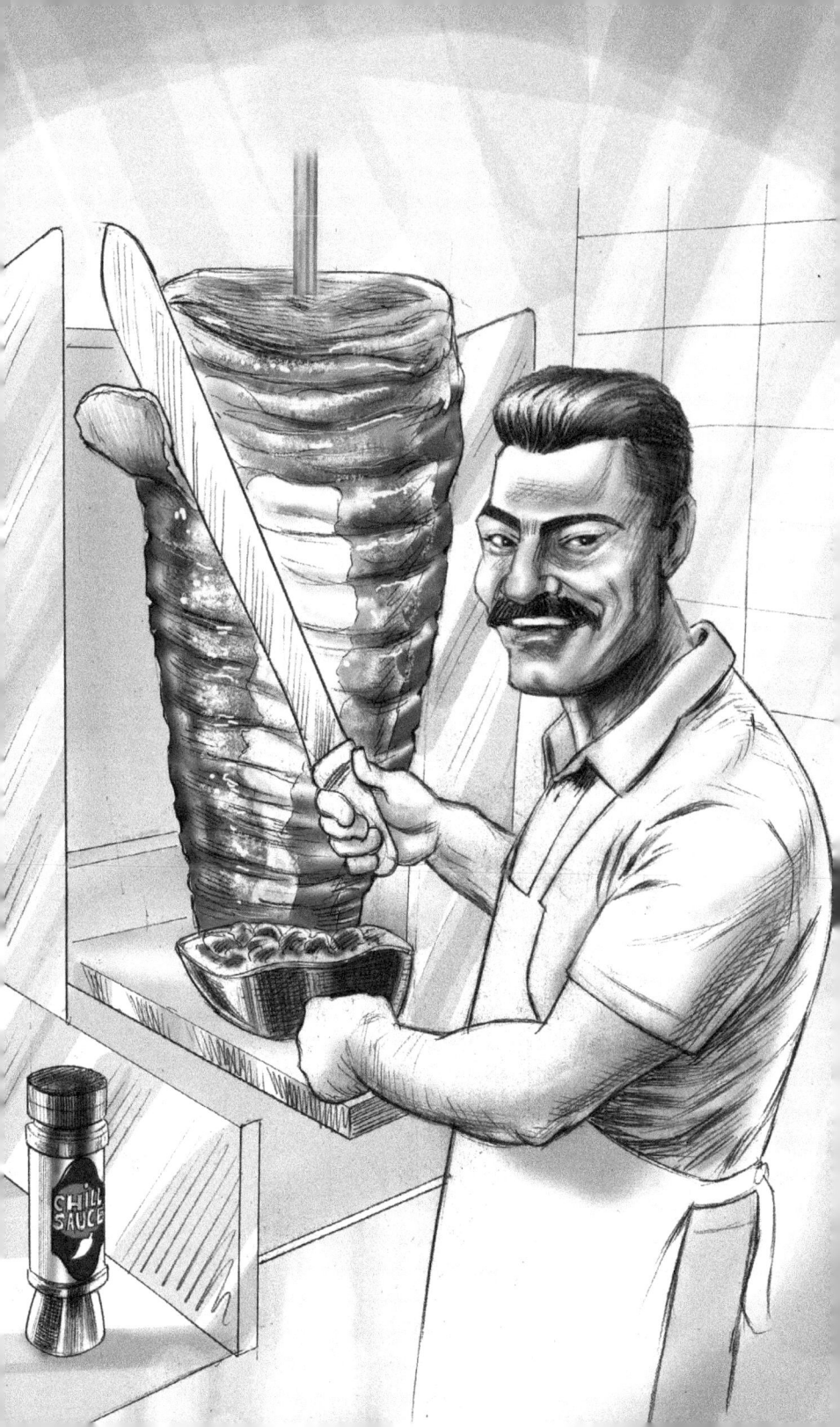

INK MY SOUL

Painful at the start,
but oh, so sweet,
a bonding experience, a merger,
finally complete.

It couldn't be more intimate.
We have longevity.
These tales of my ink,
I'll share with you.

The wings of an angel
are tattooed across my back;
its gentle curves and delicate lines
form a true celestial work of art.

They unfold
in my darkest moments,
guiding me like a beacon,
keeping me on track.

The scorpion inked on my shoulder
in bold black lines
is enigmatic and strong,
my personal star sign.

It's a reminder to be loyal,
honest and open, but to remain
hidden deep beneath rocks,
guarding secrets never to be spoken.

The sword, shield, and red rose,
all entwined on my arm,
show my strength, my sensitivity,
in its delicate charm.

It's a sign of heartbreak
and hope for future love.
May it never discolour, fade,
or come to any harm.

These marks on my skin,
a soul's cartography,
are a journey of self-expression
in ink, a bold anthology.

I dream to fly, to fight, to love,
as the stars align,
embarking on a life where
heart and spirit entwine.

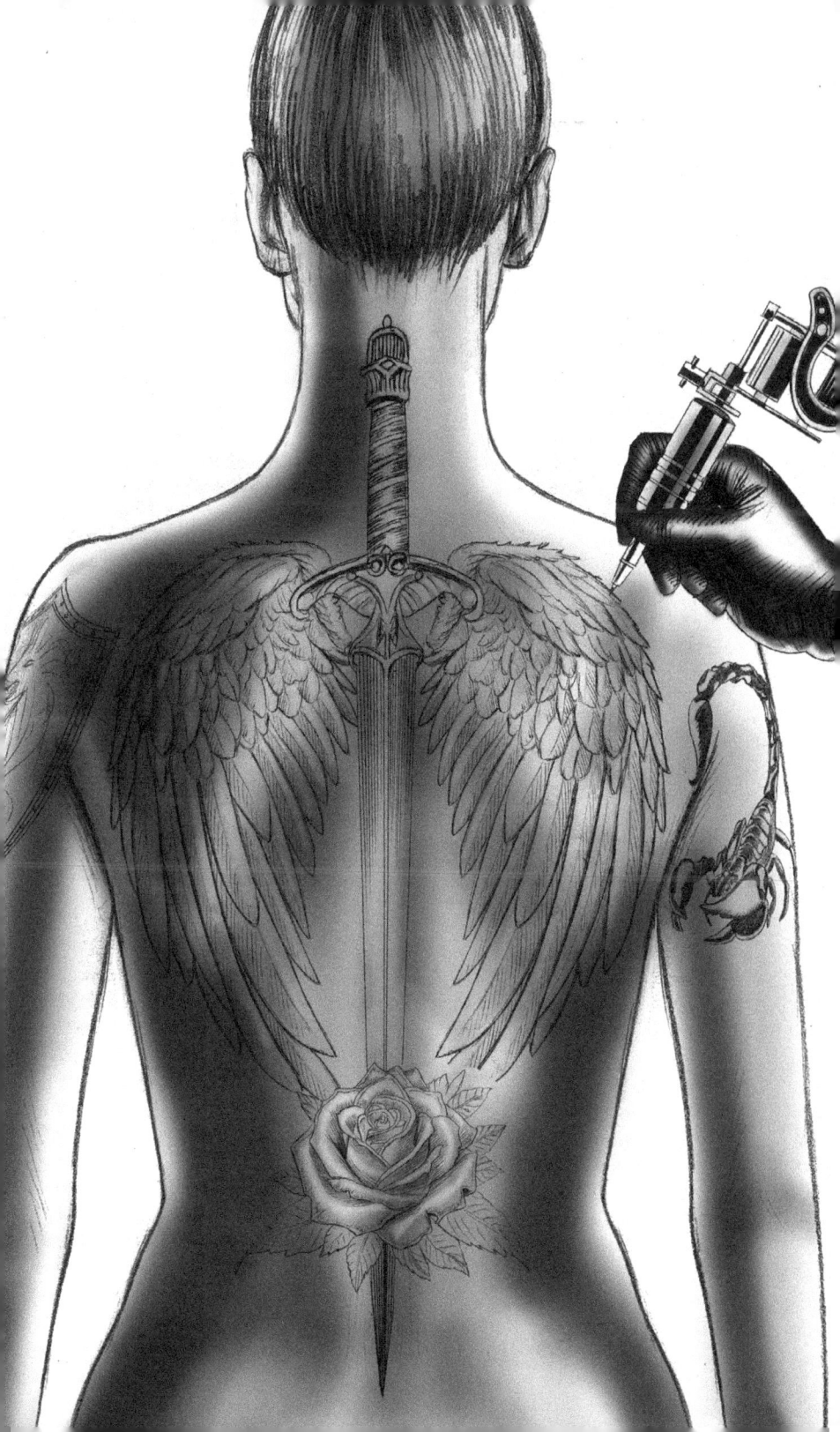

MAN OR MOUSE

Maybe this unexpected turn of events
provides a route to something much more intense.
I was dating her young daughter,
with waves of brown hair,
when her mother approached me
without any care.

She offered me a cigarette
with her manicured hand,
a test I politely declined.
'Not for me,' I replied.

Her smiling persisted:
'How about a Tennessee whisky
to help you unwind?'
I held firm, 'No thanks,
that's not my style.'

She looked me up and down,
and, with a sarcastic tone, moaned:
'Are you a man or a mouse?'
So forthright.

Baffled at first, I determinedly replied,
'I may not drink or smoke,
but I'm a passionate man
with a taste for finer things,
like your daughter's loving hand.'

She pondered a moment and smiled,
with a glint in her eye, whispering to me,
'We could ski the French Alps, you and I.'

I thanked her for the random offer,
laughing at the suggestion,
for I knew where my heart truly lay,
without a doubt or question!

But later, I pondered,
would spending time with her mother
really be so wrong? Surely,
my brown-haired beauty would not mind
if I just gave it a try...

We glided down the mountains, skiing so high;
the attraction was evident, I'd be foolish to deny.

Anything can happen when two souls collide.
Within that moment, I felt alive.

Reaching the bottom, rosy-cheeked and all smiles,
I knew this adventure was all worth the while.

We threw snowballs and kissed,
catching snowflakes in our mouths.

Her tongue was a flame, warm and inviting amid the ice.
As we kissed, the snow beneath us melted to slush.

Life can be an unexpected ride, I've learned,
and in these moments, one should relax and enjoy the
highs.

A bizarre situation. What was I supposed to do?
I was dating the daughter, and now the mother, too.

THE FALLACY OF LUXURY

GOLDEN GALA

The night breeze kisses my cheek, as if to say, 'Well done!'
It fills me with worthiness for this life, unmatched by
any other night.

I am standing on the bridge, enjoying the canal.
Lights pirouette on the water, entertaining me as boats
glide by.

Dear Amsterdam, city of dreams and bicycles,
I raise my glass and thank you, the chosen one.

Among the winding alleys and cobblestone streets,
you have a charm; no other city can compare.

But tonight, you shine brighter than ever before,
as the Gala of Gold and glamour beats at your core.

Dressed in my tuxedo, my wife stunning in gold,
we head to the film premiere, a sight to behold.

The Pathé Tuschinski Theatre welcomes us both,
as we float from a black limousine onto a carpet of gold.

Everything glitters as we are greeted with champagne.
The bubbles dance and models in golden bikinis prance.

The city dwellers adorn themselves in their finest attire.
Dutch celebrities grace the scene, lighting the night sky
like fire.

Anticipation fills the air for the silver screen,
to unveil their creation, a film-maker's dream.

SUCCESS!

On stage I stand, receiving adulation
from a packed crowd, one full of admiration.

At this moment, everything is perfect,
as if Amsterdam was created just for tonight.

The film, *The Devil's Double*, has captured their hearts.
Their seal of approval is given, without doubt.

The party rages on; the night is young.
Paparazzi cameras flash, capturing each moment's spark.

But amid the chaos, one sound rings clear:
the crowd chanting my name, evoking a smile, ear to ear.

Goosebumps dance on my skin: pure exhilaration,
a tangible reminder of this unforgettable occasion.

This is the pinnacle of hard work and longing.
Tonight, this dream soars over canals flowing in gold.

Nights like these are precious gifts, my crown.
I feel worthy of life, a golden gala in the heart of
Amsterdam.

Gala Night

HUNT HERMÈS AND MORE

You look very Parisian, darling,
in your Hermès grey-belted kaftan,
but was it worth the three-and-a-half grand?

I bought it, honey,
to match your William Hunt grey suit,
the two-tone one,
in which you look ever so cute!

Where is my bronze Berluti tie, dear,
the Scritto double-faced one?

It's in my Chanel bag, sweetie,
but I'm afraid it is all creased up!

Why did you place it among your stuff?

Sorry, I was in a rush and my mind seized up.
I'm off to Milan, and my flight's at six.

Well, just behave, sweetie, and get back quick!

I guess my Prada tobacco suede jacket
will have to suffice.

Yes, it would match my Loro Piana Nestor coat
real nice!

But... that's over fourteen thousand pounds!

MALE MODEL

I'm tall, dark and handsome,
with deep-blue diamond eyes.
I'm sexy, seductive and classy,
and I know they see the same.
Shyly, they all feast on me
and do not feign surprise
when my oozing gaze undresses
them eye to eye.

My strong, angular jaw
is square as a Rubik's Cube,
and my dazzling smile
is as wide as Broadway itself.
I enjoy a cocktail lifestyle,
consorting with only the best.

Amassing followers on social media,
with my muscles on display,
on Instagram, TikTok,
X, and Facebook,
I entice those willing
to come and play!

In a tailored Savile Row suit,
I am sophisticated, suave, and slick,
donning brushed leather

jeans and boots for a more wildly
rugged and adventurous look.

I leave nothing to the imagination,
with my toned glutes, quads, and pecs.
Some say I have a Neanderthal mentality,
but I'm just being a pest,
a bloke who's not quite ready,
for the knacker's yard just yet.

SIMPLE MAN

I'm just a simple man, with love for simple things.
Fishing and composing, is what makes my heart sing.

I live in Mouse Cottage, on the corner of Silver Street,
a quaint little abode, charming and so sweet.

Days are spent by the river, where peace and tranquillity exist,
casting lines and waiting, with each catch and release.

My lures are my art, dancing on the lines;
with vibrant hues and colours, they completely mesmerise.

My mind aligns beats and bars as I patiently wait,
orchestrating rhymes as the fish ably slip away.

Fish may not have come my way today, but I still created art,
and composed a basic melody to work on, from the heart.

As the evening falls, after supper and a cup of tea,
I'll sit at my piano and assemble today's new harmony.
You see, I'll keep on fishing and composing;
my melodies have no bounds in *poesie*,

from classical to country, jazz and even pop,
as I'm a simple man, with no idea when to stop.

URBAN RATS

I can't adapt to be an urban rat,
in this concrete jungle so densely packed.
Amid the chaos, I'd struggle to breathe,
in a city that would consume me,
like a suffocating nocuous disease.

I won't be blinded by material gain,
Rolexes, Lamborghinis, or shipwrecked champagne.
I appreciate the simple things I obtain;
true fulfilment arises in my own lane.

Urban rats on the monotonous daily grind—
tightly stacked in tunnels, they soldier on, blind.
In grey suits and ties, with hair tied back,
they seek financial security, ambition, to be Top Rat.

I can't be just another cog in the clock,
endlessly spinning like a spinning top
or mundanely running on the wheel for rats,
a common Sisyphus in never-ending plight.

No! I cannot adapt to be an urban rat,
scurrying in this concrete prison,
after drummed-up hopes and expectations
of bonuses, annual holidays, a sizable pension.

My days are not filled with meetings and deadlines,
I have the freedom to do whatever I like.
Let urban rats seek fortune and fame;
my happiness is living life, without any shame.

Break free from the race; don't be a rat.
Find your own pace and never look back.
Don't be a slave to society's demands, say
fuck off! to the corporate grind.

For no chains of ambition, no cages of gold,
break free from the script society has sold.
In defiance, I dance under the wide-open sky,
for in this vast expanse, my soul learns to fly.

SANTOS

Santos: a spectacle in our midst,
cloaked in style, his soul a swirling mist.
His spirit is untamed, free and wild,
for whom I stood in defiance, a steadfast child.

Others mocked, judged, and sneered,
'odd, weird,' in total disdain, unable
to understand his uniqueness and pain.
But beneath his charming façade
lay a darkness hidden from sight.

An estranged father he hardly knew
left emotional wounds that refused to heal.
Santos wasn't a villain, but a troubled soul,
the anger of dejection taking its toll.

He was no hero, his words often fuelled,
disrespecting his mother, showing zero gratitude.
He told her to leave, in a hurtful way,
though this woman raised him with love.
It pained me to see.

Years bonded and wove us in a tapestry
of Elvis tunes and American flicks.

His mantra, 'Stay in the movies,'
remained our philosophy, still shaping me today.

He had slicked-back hair, eyes a borrowed blue,
eyebrows shaped, fake tan, and braces.
Crisp white shirts opened wide,
revealing Jesus on a gold chain, resting on his chest,
an influence from his Spanish mother's religious quest.

Life with Santos was a kaleidoscope of the surreal.
Speeding in his black Lancia Beta Spyder car,
in nightclubs and under streetlights we would thrive—
two teenage dreamers living life, keeping it alive.

He showed me how to stand alone,
in bold defiance of conformity's throne.
To live like a movie, with a hero's grace,
to not take it too seriously, to embrace each phase.

We were the heroes of our stories,
daring to chase dreams and take risks,
ignoring doubts, silencing critics, and forging our own
paths.

He once took me by complete surprise,
recording a vinyl record with his jaw-dropping voice.

We seized life's reins with fervent hands,
savouring each moment's fleeting sands.

Despite these adventures, his familial disdain reigned,
the wedge that ego hammered
soured our friendship and continued to grow
until I bid him farewell, the ending long ago foretold.

It's been a lifetime since I've last seen him,
but I can't help but wonder what could have been;
had he found his inner potential,
instead of imitating the heroes of the silver screen.

Years later, after a predictable turn,
Santos was homeless, broken and alone.
Our paths may never cross again,
but his impact on me, I'll always hold dear.

Walking the red carpets, his velvet voice still
echoes in my head, *'Stay in the movies, Mem.'*
To which I reply, *'Santos, you were more than just
a friend.*
You were a character to behold until the very end.'

His influence on me is forever preserved.

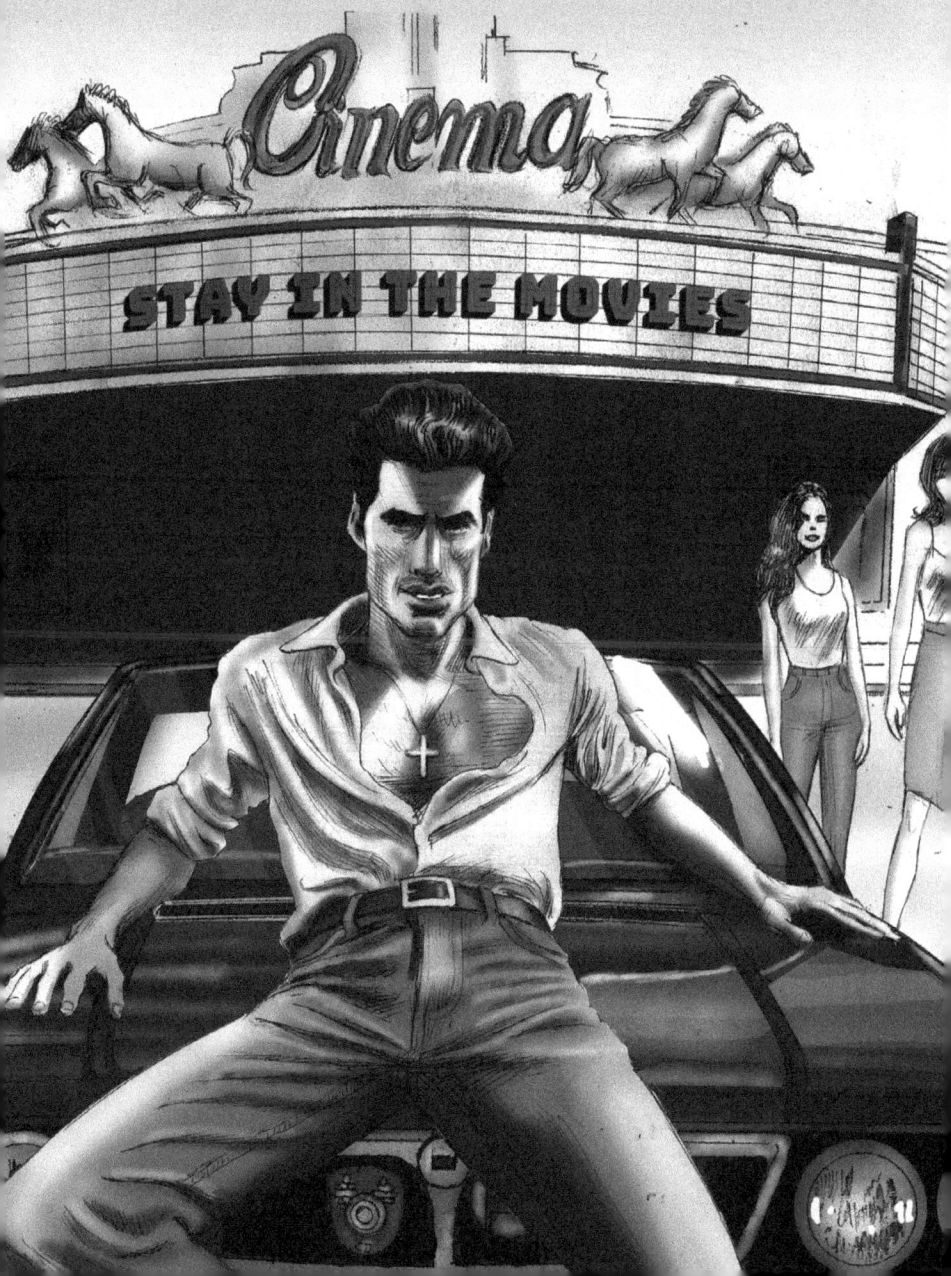

Cinema

STAY IN THE MOVIES

SURVIVING HOLLYWOOD

Sinking in quicksand, incarcerated in this fame game!
Unforgiving. My soul consumed. I was invincible;
    a star I became.
Reality stalled and hoodwinked me into believing
    I am grand.
Vicodin and the devil's lettuce met my need, as did
    crack when planned.
It all went to my head, this constant attention; I believed I was
    above all mention.
VIP, a superstar, simply the best... but, inside, I felt an
    utterly dismal mess.
Injecting to numb the pain of this life, the constant pressure
    to keep up the façade.
No matter. The persona created was high maintenance;
    the media expected exemplar perfection.
Glamour: I've basked in the limelight, which left me paranoid
    and without perception.

Hoping success would bring me exultation, not a
    never-ending battle
Of mental health and addiction. The weight of my
    name, fame, and fortune left my brain rattled.
Let me step down and walk away. I don't deserve this
    amount of richness in pay.
Lost in an ostentatious world of pretentious display.
You've made me a shell of my former self, Hollywood,
    once humble and loving.
Working hard, giving my all, now I'm just a self-obsessed
    pest, worthy of nothing.
Oh, a sensation, a shining light. Best Actor, an Oscar,
    what sheer delight.
Oh, screw all that. How I yearn for a selfless pace,
    away from cameras and judging stares.
Doing away with forced smiles from unhinged stars,
    replacing normality, family, and genuine love.

THE VALBONNE

The Valbonne was the ultimate venue,
where the super-rich had seditious rendezvous.
The beautiful danced with the wealthy,
exclusively purposeful and endlessly stealthy.

The aroma of caviar and Dom Perignon was a persistent theme.
Standing as front doorman, I lived a revered dream.
Each night revealed a selective and private scene
of DJs and celebrities: a nightclubber's dream.

Where the dance floor unfailingly pulsed
and seductive bodies rhythmically convulsed.
Where money is no object to accrue,
and indulgence flashed with the night's hue.

Where the norm for all is to covet excess,
measuring status like a game of chess.
An utter utopia for the upper classes,
for the highly esteemed to clink their glasses.

It was so surreal to man the entrance door,
mouth agape at the luxury and classic splendour.
For a time, I was enthralled with reverence at the lore,
designer clothes iced with coloured diamonds galore.

Until one-night, affluent Arabs incited a squall,
insulting the Italian waiter, begging a brawl.
Because of a simple request that the waiter misunderstood,
decked in gold, the Arabs assembled their brotherhood.

A bartender tried to call me out of sight,
and as the fight broke out, my adrenalin spiked,
But duty called and I intervened with a grin,
thwarting a man who aimed for the chin.

Awash in the tumult, the thrill of the fight,
I felt pride in keeping the scene clean that night.
That sort of petty chaos bored me the most,
for I wasn't there for belligerence, but to be the host.

A week passed and the fight's thrill wore off,
which prompted the realisation – it was time to leave.
I handed in my notice and would secretly scoff
at the monied celebrities I traded for life's reprieve.

I would not meet the fate of my predecessor:
dying in a pool of blood from a shotgun drive-by,
so I bid farewell to The Valbonne as oppressor,
abandoning the chic and elite to seek a new high,
its opulence imprinted like an endless whisper.

Valbonne

THE MARCHIONESS

Traffic was heavy, my heart racing,
paralysed in a sea of red taillights.
Fear festered, growing inside—
I was going to be late for the first time!

I hate to keep others waiting;
it's a thought I cannot abide,
but in such moments of delay,
some detours are meant to be!

Constantly checking the time,
my stomach twisted, thoughts raced,
my principled pride in punctuality
is one I endeavour to adhere to.

Watch alarm set to perfection,
route meticulously planned,
I couldn't miss this important date,
relentless in my commitment to arrive.

Freshly signed with a new agent
and flush with invitations, today's journey
led me to a birthday celebration
upon the pleasure boat, *The Marchioness*.

The traffic cleared to reveal the River Thames,
a chance to shine, to leave my mark, to ignite,
to network with unfamiliar faces and unapologetically
let loose and have fun.

I arrived at my destination, heart racing in anticipation,
and pure elation, immediately to learn
it was too late. *The Marchioness* had left,
my fate secured as she slowly unmoored.

Her lights twinkled like distant stars,
a silhouette of missed chances.
The night's embrace turned cold with regret,
sorrow seeding in my veins.

I stood there, consumed in thought and frustration,
angry at the traffic for spoiling the sublime.
The empty dock's creaking whine mocked me,
the ship's departure echoing in my mind.

Arriving home, weary and worn, I retired to bed,
contemplating: if only I had left a moment sooner,
I would now be on that deck, mingling, drinking,
where stars and city lights intersect.

Sleep would not take my anxiety;
tossing, turning, and yearning for
deep slumber, my eyes fluttered,
heavy and tired, yet my mind refused to rest.

I switched on the television news,
my heart heavy as a lead weight,
each word a bullet fired at my mind.
The news I saw, I could barely comprehend!

Numbness took hold as I tried to make sense of it all.
The Marchioness had met a terrible fate,
struck by the ruthless dredger, *Bowbelle*.
Fifty-one lives were lost in that tragic moment, a sorrowful state.

Closing my eyes, I took a sudden, chasmic breath.
I had just escaped death!
Rushing to the scene,
the bustling streets now lay silent,
a quiet testament to fate's sharp turn.

On the embankment, my heart sank with grief,
a mere witness of the aftermath on the Thames,
once serene, now littered with debris.
Hot tears poured and scorched my cheeks.

I could have been among the victims of this pain,
but fate intervened, and I was spared.
Emotions flooded through me as I realised
my overwhelming gratitude for that delay.

The traffic that seemed like a curse was now a blessing
in disguise, shielding me from death and dreams
heart-wrenchingly shattered, a true tragedy
that left all the survivors battered.

With a heavy heart, I pen these lines, a
homage to souls departed on that sombre night.
A reminder of life's unpredictable currents, and the
preciousness of moments, fleeting yet bright.
On 20th August 1989, I learnt to embrace life's
unpredictable flow.

MEMISMs

My name is Mem, a name unique, very short and, often told, sweet.
In the recesses of my mind, I formulate MEMISMs: Philosophy
created by words and my disposition, the essence of my kingdom.
I call them MEMISMs, my ethics and doctrine to champion life
and navigate with wisdom through any strife, to shape reality
by power of thought; fundamentally, we become what we think we ought!
Life is fugacious, it must be lived now! MEMISMs will help you
understand "how". We all have four fingers and a thumb—
together they make a perfect sum. So here are five MEMISMs
to give you a helping hand and guide you the best they can.
First comes the pointer finger, stable and true.

MEMISM One

Stand up tall, arms outstretched wide,
now slowly embrace yourself with all your flaws inside,
for they are what make you truly unique.
Welcome them and let your unfeigned self shine through.
Next is the middle finger, often misunderstood,
an erratic gesture, often thought rude.

MEMISM Two

In this world of social media and MEMISMs,
the contacts app becomes our prism.
Open the contacts app on your mobile phone,
and click delete on all past friends you've known.
You're not rude or showing disdain,
it's about breaking free from old chains.
Expunge the toxic and hold onto the strong.
Next is the ring finger, symbol of love and commitment.

MEMISM Three

Let us not only pledge our love to one special person,
but spread love far and wide, unconditionally,
and to every needing human; for every time we give,
it will return, tenfold, a cycle that will never recede or turn cold.
Next, the little "pinky" finger, with its power to connect and inspire.

MEMISM Four

At nightfall when the sky is adorned with resplendent stars,
look up at the velvet sky and allow your mind to meander for inspiration.
Your dreams will amplify, inflaming your imagination, of this I'm certain.
Finally, the thumb. The opposable digit, signalling all is fine.

MEMISM Five

As you awaken with each break of dawn, make an affirmation
and verbalise:

Live each day with passion and zest.
Trust your heart as it knows best.
Don't be afraid of an unknown path.
I'm capable and strong, for goodness' sake.

These handful of MEMISMs embolden me to "live in the moment",
to "embrace the unknown", to "love with all my heart", as I adventure through life. May they enthuse you, too, to live life and love it with all its imperfections and beautiful sights.

SOCIETY

FORTY-TWO NIGHTS (DAMNED SLEEP)

(Gunning Ward – St. George's Hospital)

Regimented observations
come every fourth hour,
with monitors bleeping,
echoing their constant reminder.

Forty-two nights laid on my back,
no turning left or right,
a gutter frame beside me,
a commode clear in sight.

Damn, I need some sleep
to help aid my fight!

Time for the concoction,
a paragon of painkilling drugs.
Paracetamol's phantom kiss,
dihydrocodeine's hazy embrace,
and morphine's siren song
lure me to oblivion tonight.

With fingertip pinned in a pulse oximeter
and thermometer probing my mouth,
arms strapped to measure blood's pressure,

another sleepless night
escapes me in my plight!

Curtains are hurriedly drawn:
a new victim has arrived.
Privacy is a failed seclusion.
Each word is audible in fright:

'FUCKING LET ME OUT OF HERE.'

I hear the nearby inmate cry,
shattering the fragile quiet.
It's a sentiment that vibrates
in the caverns of my chest,
as I, too, am of that mind.

Damn, I need some sleep!
Please pray that I just might!

ON THE BORDER OF NORTH MACEDONIA

On the border of North Macedonia,
border police keep their bastard sniffer dogs at their side
for sport.
My bloody ticket to ride, they inexorably snatch my
passport.
Journey impaired, I'm detained with no fucking idea why.

Restraining me under the suspicion of trafficking drugs,
true dystopia!
The hurl me into lock-up, smeared in excrement for
night's fort.
Laying in a cell, darkness engulfing me like a thick fog
with no other resort.
On the border of North Macedonia.

I know my innocence, my strength, and my faith will bring
euphoria.
Yet trapped in this senseless dungeon, a fate I cannot
abort,
unmarred, cocksure, and consummate – my resolve will
not contort.
Justice prevailed the next day; I was freed, without
fanfare from the myopia,
on the border of North Macedonia.

ALLOW THE SILENCE

Leaders stand at the brink,

where decisions weigh heavy.

Not all are redeemable;

some paths diverge too far for crossing back,

yet in every ending lies a seed of new beginnings.

Harmony over discord,

choice over chaos,

a symphony awaiting our hands.

Free will, not dissonance,

can be achieved.

In the quiet, listen to

the world's heartbeat.

Inherent in the human condition,

we can suffocate our own

mortal existence,

with injected ideology,

ideas sharpened to knives,

commands that wound the soul.

Halt the march, catch the breath,

ponder paths yet walked.

ALLOW THE SILENCE.

A world in which

peace prevails is

a thing we'd all like to see.

We are more than a land mass—

we are a country, reconciled

coherently:

ALLOWING THE SILENCE!

FRACTURED

'Don't weep,
she is not your child,'
I plead, knelt before you.
We are fractured,
damaged by our past.

Charred trees surround us,
as lamenting mothers cry.

Death. Mourning for sanity.
Orphans bleed from shrapnel wounds,
their cries deafening the night skies,
studded with the faces of their loved ones,
parent and child.
Has persecution ravaged our hearts?

Life remains precious
for Muslims and Jews.
We hang in the balance of historical conflict.

ISLAMOPHOBIA
ANTISEMITISM

promote an agenda in such atrocity!

Let it not shame us.

Reach out your hand and say no to war.

A safe passage to peace awaits us,

fractured and fragmented as we are.

TONIGHT, I PRAY

Dwindling screams,
survivors trapped.
Be saved,
I pray.

First responders,
have strength,
provide aid!
I pray.

May the missing under rubble
be found safe,
reunited in love,
I pray.

Draw near, God,
to comfort the living,
who wail for the dead.
I begin to fray.

Livelihoods lost,
homes destroyed.
Have courage,
I pray.

May the injured
be healed and may
no one suffer alone,
I pray.

Almighty God,
may this heartache and sorrow
never, ever be repeated.
Tonight, I pray.

WRAP ME IN SILVER FOIL

Wrap me in silver foil,
as I am walking wounded.
Regulate my body temperature,
I beg of you. Shield me
before I succumb to the same fate
of the fifty-two souls solemnly departed.
I have witnessed the malignant,
vile pit of human... kind!

Seven hundred and sixty-nine souls maimed,
disfigured, and traumatised.
I am victim seven hundred and seventy,
a number for a nameless face,
in this merciless harsh reality
where cries are silenced and tears solitary,
from actions humanity inflicts on itself.

Wrap me tight in silver foil,
quivering like a marathon runner,
on this concrete bed as deep pain
seeps into every bone, a paramedic
succouring my desperate need.

I repudiate becoming
just another statistic,

a life undone,
taken by a cause,
hateful, deviant
and contorted,
all in the purported
name of religion.

Four resolute assholes,
with malice in their vacuous hearts,
let their ruinations swarm
as they strapped bombs
dependably to their chests,
setting out to cause absolute devastation
to the bustling streets of London.

The targets of their hate
were bus and underground stations,
packed with innocent souls,
unaware of their impending damnation,
on that doomy, ominous day:
the 7th of July, 2005.

The damage is unfathomable
as the smoke clears,
outright chaos in Aldgate,
Edgware Road, and Russell Square.
Thirty-nine guiltless lives callously claimed.
A fourth device detonates
with a deafening sound
in a diverted double-decker bus,

calling thirteen more angels Heaven-bound.
London wept as the news spread.
True spirits of humanity emerged—
strangers helping, holding each other
in a show of solidarity. The heroes
whose courage surged stood tall,
for they had risked their lives to save all.

The bombers left a nation of broken hearts,
their minds blind with hate and twisted delusion,
calling themselves 'soldiers' of their higher power—
a mangled, rogue version of Islam, so wrong,

What justification can there be
for the execution of innocents
in the name of deity?
No religion
preaches
hate!

Unwrap me from this silver foil, cast it away.
Let me not succumb to its grasp, for I am stronger.
Terrorism is real, but united
we will weave diverse beliefs
to find peace in our shared humanity.
Let us remember the lost,
honour them with every breath,
for in their memory animosity ceases,
as we see the world through love's depth.

GO AWAY, COVID

Before you came, we'd get into our car
and drive for hours to somewhere far.

We had no worry of lockdowns or assigned slots to shop,
no concern of the possibility we might be stopped.

Before you came, we'd find a secluded place
where we could relax, kiss, and fully embrace.

No anxiety while hand-washing, *Did I do it right?*
Or paranoia while holding you against me, tight.

Before you came, we would meet with friends,
warm and snug, with drink and laughter without end.

Not abiding to the rule of two metres apart,
or scrutinising the brand of each other's mask!

Before you came, we would visit our family
whenever we'd like, deigning the dressing

of hazmat suits and gloves, or climbing into a crane
to wave through glass, our goodbyes.

We've buried our loved ones without letting them
properly depart,
as you infected our minds as well as our hearts.

Spirits that cannot be killed are enlivened,
persistent,
in our way of life, merely disrupted by your futile
existence.

Humanity will be the victorious one,
demolishing you once our vaccines are done.

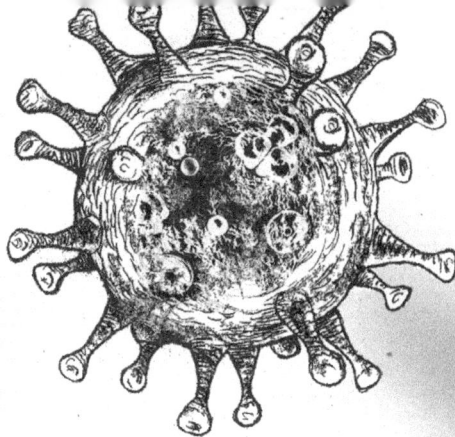

VACCINE ONSLAUGHT

The pharmacist, late, hastily set up the chairs,
turning to smile as I walked in the door.

She said in a singsong: 'Come in and take a seat,'
calming her anxious demeanour.

I waited, yet knowing the truth
no vaccine would make me bulletproof.

It's just a temporary fix; the virus will mutate,
finding a new way to infiltrate.

Chaos builds as people filter in,
another vaccine onslaught about to begin.

Lines of anxious hearts, hoping for protection,
fearing they'll be torn apart by the pandemic infection.

The price of modern medicine skyrockets,
as well-being is monetised, sold, and delivered.

Four jabs in a few months, we are told,
Pfizer, Moderna, Sputnik V and AstraZeneca.

Surely it's enough, or perhaps not?
With no end in sight, she calls me up,

I ask, 'Which vaccine?' To no reply, except,
'Please roll up your sleeves! Jab!'

'Your booster is done, hun!' Hurriedly,
she hands me a card. 'Be sure to fill in your name!'

My inner voice questions, *Did I really need another shot?*
Or is my mind playing a deceitful plot?

A red sore flares where the needle went in.
Feeling fatigued, head pounding, I turn on the radio news.

'Omicron variant detected in the UK!'

My shoulder still throbbing from the recent jab,
I'm screaming inside, *Not another strain; when will it end?*

CALMING SEA

Calming sea, come envelop me
in your welcoming embrace, let me be.
With your tranquil waters, soothe my soul,
quench my body's thirst and make me whole.

Whisk me away to a state of ease,
soothing me with your north-easterly breeze.
Glistening and shimmering in the sunlight heat,
your warmth on my eyelids, makes me feel complete.

Your beauty lies beyond what I can see.
I am but a speck in this expanse, so free.
As I float in your arms, my worries all cease,
drifting from reality to serenity in peace.

Pearls of salt upon my lips sedate me;
your waves' rhythm is like a lullaby, heavenly.
On your tide, my spirits lift to a sleep so serene;
under spangling stars, I repose and dream.

CLOUDS THAT THUNDER

Behemoth clouds rumble with mighty growls
and dark winds chant a melancholic tune.
They paint the sky like a canvas of gloom,
manifesting in a sorrowful scowl
and harmonious with a mournful howl.
Though they roar, clouds that thunder seldom rain—
it's not always the aim of cyclic strains.
No thunderhead bestows its droplets now.

Beneath the storm, I marvel at their might;
like fearsome beasts, they leisurely depart,
teasing and taunting as they roll and stir.
The sky, draped black, is abducted of light,
mirroring the shadows within my heart,
mixed with a bittersweet pain, now a blur.

FIREARM ISTANBUL

Minarets
and baklava,
markets of gold and leather—
there I sat in the taverna,
with a firearm pointing at my nether
as the imam called worshippers to prayer.

LOVE

I CARE NOT FOR ANYTHING ELSE

Today marks the anniversary
of the day we first met,
a significance like no other,
one I'll never, ever forget.

The world may be in lockdown,
but we are safeguarded by our shield,
the one our love created—
robust, resilient, and sealed.

Tonight, let's venture to the balcony
and fill the tranquil night
with echoes of drunken laughter
and sweet chortles of our past.

No politicians, no socialites,
no woke or cancel culture,
no racism, no sexism
can interfere. It's just love and us.
I care not for anything else.

Your fingertips softly ruffle
the strands of my hair.
Your alluring fragrance draws me close
as I calmly declare:

'I love you,'
in the early morning dew.
I feel blessed by another day with you,
and am eagerly anticipating
every tomorrow coming anew.

The next anniversary, and the next,
reminds me of the first,
each immortalising that magical day
when I met you.
I care not for anything else.

FIRST LOVE

Beauty lay in simplicity with you, in your electric-blue
shirt and faded jeans,
in art and film study. My leading lady, you provided a
captivating view,
with cat-like eyes and luscious lips... my Bond girl; my
Raquel Welch; my dream.

Our lips would meet like a sweet addiction, her taste
a perfect duo
on my tongue of Pernod and blackcurrant (her
signature drink),
making my heart unfurl in complete submission.

Skipping class to nestle in the cinemas' darkness,
we watched *Endless Love* for the sixth time,
and as the screen flickered, your head would rest on
my shoulder, and we merged into one.
We navigated this labyrinth of intimacy until its moment
of closure.

You'd lend me your perfumed scarf, to fill my senses
and cast your spell
like a smoothing balm, lulling me into a velvet cocoon,
helping me sleep.
Oh, my Mauritian temptress; in your beauty, I was
repaired, my soul was well.

I felt satiating pleasure walking in Clapham Common,
    your hand in mine,
our world created among emblazoned flowers in
    bloom.
As we journeyed to dine, I wished our love would
    never end.

Like a puzzle scattered wide, our love was complex,
    involved and finally scarred.
I still remember our first kiss. You were my first real love.
In my heart, you'll remain a safeguarded memory I'll
    never discard.

A CHERUBIC AFFAIR

In the comfort room of our work arena,
you whispered in my ear,
crimson lips abutting my lobe, adrenalising my heart
from an embittered relationship, a chance encounter.
Deviously wrong until that fateful embrace,
we called action for the soap opera of turbulence,
each abandoning our lovers.

Our sexual intimacy was a wild, crazed euphoria of
never-ending screwing, on the kitchen table in candlelight.
Amid passionate intercourse, onlookers eyeballed.
It didn't bother us; we were completely enthralled.

My flirting ways in the workday maze upset you.
Drinking behind the wheel, you were hell-bent on running
        me over.
Forgiving your fury, I escaped with you to Birmingham,
where a fortune teller read our fate, predicting its end.

Defying all odds, we proved naysayers wrong.
Your stepfather fretted about the age gap,
resolute our affair was built on shifting sand!
Your mother, a true sweetheart, was never judgmental.
She believed and reassured us, bless her.

We romanticised plans about a daughter,
calling her Cherub, a symbol of our forbidden love
and our fatuous fantasy. We deceived ourselves,
deep in sex, denying the story's inevitable end.
Now, we both have fulfilling families;
our story has ended, cherished between us
only in memory.

JUST GO

I sense your thoughts
piercing my already-punctured heart.
I can't give any more.
Just go if you must!

You clipped our wings
with resolute new beliefs,
dragging our commitments
through the mud.

True love in fragments,
a dishonoured past,
a relationship blackened
by the dust of mistrust.

You chose dishonesty,
saying you had no other love.
Accept our parting—
no repentance, no return.

BRIDE

Dripped in wet desire,

the bride in her white silk dress,

so warm to the touch.

FRANCESCA SCARLET AND RUPERT HENRI

Francesca Scarlet, my feline queen, and Rupert Henri,
   a king in cat form.
With simple elegance and lovingness, they grace my
   home.
Their presence in my life is a blessing. With personalities
   so different,
but in harmony always, they tread in unison across
   my abode.

Francesca's emerald eyes gleam against her beautiful
   tabby coat;
like a Hollywood starlet, she moves with true poise
   and finesse.
A leading lady in every sense, each step is assertive,
   magnetic.
With a flick of her tail, she mesmerises with purring
   symphonies of seduction.

I'm convinced she is Marilyn Monroe reincarnated,
   bewitching all
as Rupert Henri stands by her side, regal and proud,
   with a snow-white fur
and golden glimmering eyes. Protecting Francesca
   with a fiery spirit,

he prowls like a monarch throughout the house
	and rules
over the garden, with no dissension from
	neighbourhood cats.

But amid his strength lies a feather-light heart, as he
	curls up with
Francesca for the night. His lion demeanour now
	is sombre and innocent,
snuggled, side by side, in their cosy little nook. Their
	love for each other
is clear in every look, his pensive gaze so evocative of
	Aristotle's deep maze.
His mind is sharp and keen; the epitome of feline
	philosophy.

Oh, how I love my two different souls, from different times.
One, a seductress, her star presence so light; the
	other, a thinker, with
a mind so bright. They may be just cats to the world
	outside, but, to me,
they are reincarnations of great minds— together,
	happy and carefree.

Unexpectedly, Francesca fell ill in the winter months.
The light that shone so bright dulled. My heart
imploded. I tried,
but nothing could prevent my pretty queen as she
flew to Heaven, up high.
With heavy hearts, we reluctantly said our goodbyes.

Left behind was Rupert, his head gloomily bowed and the once-shimmering,
gold-speckled eyes, now lifeless. His handsome whiskers drooped and
his meows were voiceless. Each day grew longer without his mate,
mourning Francesca, as his health began to fade. It wasn't long before dear
Rupert Henri met the same fate, joining Francesca in cat heaven, side by side.

They were not just cats, you see, but companions, family, so loving and free.
Their love for each other and me, is forever in my heart, eternally.

COMPANION OF WAR

Dark skies
will brighten once again.
The bombs that fall near
will finally disappear.

To the rumble in the night sky,
I say, 'Be silent,'
hugging my Shiba Inu dog,
her sombre eyes fixed to mine.

'It will pass,'
I promise her,
stroking her fur.

'You will jump, run,
and joyfully play.
Beside my bed,
you will lounge and lay.'

Believe in me,
my most
trusted
and loyal friend,
how I'll love you
till the very end!

LOVE KISMET

Alabaster-sculpted
cheekbones,
ocean-blue eyes
and skin of soap...
I could spend a lifetime praising
this Heaven-sent love, Kısmet.

Through aggressive winds
and fallen olive trees,
I'm resting upon this dream.
She's the Ying to my Yang.
There's no doubt
I'll love her endlessly.

Enchanted moments together
are as many as scattered autumn leaves,
unfurling from the bud of which
I consigned my fate,
and she willingly agreed.

Cellularly, from my entire being,
I will cherish and protect,
defeating death
with love's immortality.

The black, silken cloth
that once covered my eyes
lifts to reveal you
as a million shimmering
diamonds, my love, Kısmet.

SIMPLEST TRUTH

Now you return, mind mended, claiming peace.
Fifteen summers cannot erase the strife.
The roots of hurt bind us, yet they may cease.
Your words once cut deep, like a knife.

No reason given, no morals to stand on.
Metamorphosed spinelessly, you turned your back.
Brotherhood's bond, you could not understand.
The forgiveness you seek is impossible to hack.

But brothers once more, we find solace in view,
amends made, tormented bonds now steadfast.
The hurtful memories die in situ.
Together, our spirits thrive— our ties are vast.

Forgiveness can heal the inconceivable.
A brother's bond deepened and is now agreeable.

THE FOREST

I lit a joint upon returning
to the forest
where we walked,
hand in hand
and in love.
I drew on it hard,
swirling smoke around me
like a lover's embrace.
I spun to let the dizziness take hold,
the world blurring into a blue haze.

Closing my eyes,
I found myself transported to the past,
my soul consumed,
hidden from prying eyes.
I wondered if other hearts
would find this world as we did.

I loved how the rustling leaves
whispered our names
as the trees kissed
in the distant breeze.
In this enchanted space,
we stood and talked,
as the forest listened in
and heard our hearts.

The autumn rain descended,
a gentle cascade, like pearls of elation,
as our bodies became tangled.
Beneath the boughs,
we surrendered our souls.

We climaxed together
among the tall trees,
which stood like sentinels,
guarding the velvety green ground
where we lay.

We were frozen,
lost in each other's gaze,
as the white falcon soared above,
in the mist, seeking its prey.
The running stream witnessed
our love.
I prayed our flame would never fade
and forever remain.

On this return,
with a heavy heart,
my eyes filled with tears,
seeking solace amid the ferns.
The spot we ignited our love flame
was stamped out,
only the ashes bearing our names.

The trees still stood,
the birds still sang,
but without you... it meant nothing.
My tears fell like raindrops
to kiss the ground,
knowing our sacred place was no more.
As I walked through the paths
we roamed, I was alone.

The sun doesn't shine
as brightly now that we're apart.
I romanticised this forest
as a symbol of our love,
but shattered love
is a delicate thing.

I decided to leave, to forget this place,
and turned my back to bid farewell
to our once-perfect love.

Acceptance is hard, but I can't forgive
 unfaithfulness.
I knew I must move on.
That forest, once a testament to us,
became a fragile relic of crushed trust.

GRIEF

AYDIN

How do I express this unfathomable loss, suffocating me with each deep breath. My heart has been shattered into a million irreparable pieces. Each fibre of my being aches.

'Loss' – such a feeble word – fails to capture the magnitude of the immense devastation reverberating within. My world numbed as silence deafens my senses: a sadness devoid of solace. She was the embodiment of my world, encompassing every part of my being.

My beloved sister, Aydın, was a beautiful, inspirational light, guiding me through life. She was the most precious treasure. Her name carries the meaning of being 'enlightened and bright', perfectly embodying her essence. A formidable lawyer at the tender age of twenty-six, her life was tragically cut short by the merciless hand of fate.

As I shouldered my dear sister's coffin, the sun abruptly concealed itself behind sombre clouds, the freshly turned earth overwhelming my senses with a wave of grief.

Memories of the fear-stricken months flooded my mind. A deep sorrow etched within me, as I recalled the dreary corridors and dimly lit marble staircase I ascended daily at the Royal Brompton Hospital. There was nothing 'royal' about it. Peeling paint shed from the walls, mixed with the stench of linoleum and disinfectant; a bitter cocktail, intensifying the ache in my heart.

The weight, though feather-light on my shoulder, bore down physically and emotionally, accompanied by a relentless, permeating pain. The air was heavy with sorrow. The void of my sister's absence was so palpable. The heavy grey clouds unfurled themselves as a funeral veil.

The unyielding bond we shared, abruptly severed, left me adrift in emptiness. Her melodic voice echoes in the silence of my mind, as do her gentle touch and her captivating almond-shaped brown eyes, wise beyond her years, which radiated beauty and bravery – unparalleled.

Aydın was an A student, a beacon of knowledge, as resilient in her studies as she was courageous. I imagined the consultant's dreaded words falling on my sister's innocent young ears. How could she find the strength to fight? Yet fight she did, with a ferocity that would shame a gladiator.

I arrived at the graveside, my palms and forehead drenched in sweat, my mind transported to that fateful day.

Her absence is painfully evident. Where once her affectionate smile, gracing delicate porcelain features, met me with tenderness each day, now her almond-shaped eyes are gently shut, her head slightly tilted, pressing worryingly on my senses.

At the hospital, my father slumped in a defeated heap, cradling her feet in his trembling hands, reassuring Mum her feet were warm to the touch. Mum caressed Aydın's hair lovingly, saying "But her cheeks felt ice cold!" Was she sleeping? If only...

Oh, Aydın...

I clung to the cold, steel bedframe, its icy touch seeping into my flesh. The blinding whiteness of the floor and walls clashed in a jarring assault. Disorientated, the walls closed in on me with a crushing, unfamiliar wave of claustrophobia.

I turned to Mum; scorched trails of tears lined her gentle face. Her expression contorted into a gut-wrenching shriek, piercing the depths of my spine and rattling the hospital walls, as if to reach the Heavens above. This unbearable anguish: a pain known only to a mother who has lost her child.

My father was defeated after the unwavering efforts he made consulting world-renowned experts. None offered a solution to the tumour, dangerously close to my sister's caring heart. I shivered, seeing my father broken, exhaustion and weariness etched into every line of his distinguished face.

I stared with detest at the consultant,
whose terrifying words echoed in my ears,
each syllable a dagger into my heart,
'Sorry, we did all we could.'
My mind was unable to comprehend
that this man before me, bound by an oath to preserve life, had ultimately failed – he had deceived me.

He approached me, desperate to explain and validate.
I grabbed him and pushed him up against the sterile wall. I cried, 'Please... don't!'
My voice was filled with rage and desperation.
Panic coursed through my every vein, constricting my chest. It was impossible to breathe. I had to escape. I HAD TO RUN!

I didn't go home. I was lost in a haze of confusion over four endless days and nights, a blur punctuated by one vivid image – the comforting presence of two strangers walking with me through Battersea Park. Their words of understanding were a balm to my scorched soul.

A cycle of haunting nightmares and elusive dreams followed,

each day bleeding into the next.

In dreams, I saw Aydın well, awakened by my own cries after hearing Mum's downstairs, for she, too, had the same dream. Days of resentment and bitterness followed. Seeing other young girls consumed in happiness, I questioned: *Why not her? Or her? Or her? Why Aydın?*
The unfairness of it all burdened my heart, plaguing my mind,
like an anchor
dragging me deeper into the murky depths of despair. The countless religious ceremonies held at our home overwhelmed me. There were mourners, heads bowed in prayer, the sound of supplications filling the air as candles flickered and incense burned. Despite the ache in my heart, witnessing the solace it brought to my grieving parents was undeniable. The reality remained...

As we gently lowered her coffin to prayer, I recollected my beliefs that miracles could exist...
clearly not.
Equally, believing that God, the embodiment of mercy, could surely not be complicit
in the plight of someone so innocent and deserving of life as
Aydın!

A soul so unique, she exuded warmth, gentleness and care. Her beauty and selflessness were awe-inspiring. She was pure-hearted, loving and intelligent, with an aura of tranquillity that others desired to be around. Perhaps in the depths of her kind soul, Paradise always awaited her – a place where God intended her to be.

A MOTHER'S PASSING

Death had never felt so real
as it did that November day.
My heart was forcefully ripped out
and kept captive by loss,
as my vision drained
all colours seeping away.

Indeed, I am an orphan now,
in the void of unconditional love.
Those who cherished me from the moment of
birth were now stolen from up above.

My feelings were overwhelmed
by both memories and photographs.
Still, I was grateful for their blessings
and love's light along the path.

The silence of the empty bedroom
now echoes throughout the house.
Yet I feel her presence
embracing my soul, reassuring me,
all will be alright.

Like a gentle breeze, a mother's love
caresses with affection.

Her sweet kisses imprinted
on my heart and illuminated
the darkest moments.
The epitome of beauty lingers
as I yearn for more.

YOUR HURT IS GREATER

Your hurt is greater, Father, I know.
Each day, Father, defies reason.
Life's pardon gets lost to death's trespassing,
unquestioned.

In the kitchen, her absence is felt.
And her touch still lingers—
a testament in tea towels
folded with her devoted care.

Forgive my faltering heart, Father;
within your abyss, my own sorrow deepens.
Your hurt is greater than mine,
so deep that no words can convey.

Upstairs in the bedroom,
her hairbrush rests, a silent guardian
on her dressing table,
holding vigil for her return.

Father, we need your reassuring smile
to light up these dark and weary days.
In your presence, we find solace and
comfort that nothing can outweigh.

Her nightdress still hangs in the cupboard,
carrying a delicately sweet, lingering scent
of jasmine and rose, blend and twine,
whispering echoes of her charm and grace.

Her absence is a vice of pain, silencing our discourse
with the void she leaves behind.
In our sorrow, her legacy endures. She is our foundation
and our guide; her love is our constant companion.

We'll weather the challenge, Father,
for we are bound by love and blood.
Let me be your source of strength, as you are mine,
and, with unwavering courage, we'll rise above.

EVERLASTING

2018, how I longed to see you end.

The sadness you sourced, the bitterness caused,
will destructively remain.

I try to stay calm and refrain from anger
at you stealing Mum, learning to accept it's forever.

It's the cycle of life, as one would say,
which we each must pass along the way.

Am I to be silently accepting?
The sadness is said to be everlasting!

Perhaps the pain will dissipate,
as I preserve her love deep within.

I'll pray to learn to live a physical life without her;
on a spiritual journey, I'll begin.

As we entered 2019,
I banished uncertainty, replaced it with positivity,
peace, and hope.

I learned to understand survivorship,
imparting ways to gain strength to cope.

In 2019, my afflicted heart wounds were impaled
once more.
I lost my magnificent Dad.

Sadly, life is never the counsellor or giver of earthly
love;
it's often unrelenting and tempestuous, it turns out.

ARDA

How do I substantiate,
other than to ask you to understand, believe, and accept?

He was a gentle soul, radiating kindness
that would wrap around your heart with a warm tightness.

My words are sincere and honest, not painting perfection,
but showing my mind's eye of a deceased friend's affection.

We met at drama school, his smile emitting rays of cheer
across the space, captivating to all who beheld it near.

He had an honest, handsome face with a brilliant mind,
illuminating the depths of his imagination, like fireworks
        aligned.

Am I romanticising, unrealistically, our kindred past?
No. Words cannot describe his exceptionality and fail to
        make it last.

His dreams never surrendered, echoing in corridors of
        his soul.
Well-mannered dear friend, in the role of Hamlet, you
        strolled.

I remember a resounding roar erupt, a standing ovation,
filling the state theatre, a homage to his homeland,
   soil, and nation.

A call at dawn, *'I'm going to star in a movie, like you,*
   dear friend; 'Time of the Heart'
at Pera Palace Hotel, where Agatha Christie would write.'

Air filled with the excitement of potential opulence of
   fame.
A star emerged that night: Arda Kanpolat was his name.

A resplendent gala was held to honour his success.
Talented actors cheered him with no redress.

As he went for a cigarette break, the relentless press
   pursued;
with flashing cameras and hounding questions, they
   continued to intrude.

The scent of perfume and freshly polished marble
mingled with anticipation as distant voices hummed
   and garbled.

Faces contorted, twisted with pain – confusion reigned.
Tears etched tracks on skin, hands held heads up,
   strained.

What happened?

My dearest of all friends was swallowed by the darkness,
he tragically tumbled down a dimly lit, empty lift shaft,
cascading.

The national press convened, their voices a symphony
of opinion,
each word echoing through the room, filling every
crevice with conviction.

Amid the sombre whispers, the word '*Suicide*'
emerged, bold, stark, and grey.
Within me, a fire burned; a resolute certainty
prevailed. No way!

My heart is still shattered; no one knew him as well as me.
With love and youth, his heart did swell, a spirit pure
and rare, for all to see.

Fragile as blooms that grace the spring, he brought
tranquillity to all he encountered.
No inquest was actioned, but we knew the truth,
beyond the public glare, regardless.
The national press labelled him: a man lost in despair,
troubled with pain.
The interviewer pestering him on that day,
disappeared and was never seen again!

I'll never forget Arda as the fantastic, talented, and
charismatic actor
whose presence would light up any stage, no matter
the benefactor.

I'll cherish every memory of our friendship, true and
    flawless,
lingering like the scent of freshly cut roses, only
    endless.

BROOKWOOD

the rain had ceased.
A deep resonance calls me,
stirring inside, impossible to ignore.

as we arrived, with a sense of trepidation,
a sullen darkness loomed
despite the sun's glare.

scattered leaves hinted at decay,
discoloured in rustic brown
and orange shades.

slightly ajar, weathered gates creaked,
a reminder of neglect
yearning for rejuvenation.

my heart battled, echoing in my ears,
as a malignant tumour rose
deep in my throat.

a dense sigh escaped my lips
as i clutched the holy book for strength and light,
its weight an anchor in my turmoil.

the base of my mother's grave
was adorned with delicate flowers,
yet their beauty belied the emptiness, a void.

as my hands touched the cold granite,
the morning breeze, like mum's embrace
caressed my tear-streaked face.

i wanted to protect her from the cold,
where spirits cope.
i longed to envelop her in warmth and safety.

incense sticks were lit and placed
beside vibrant lilies, their loveliness
evoking a sense of peace.

i read a prayer of grace,
speaking of a mother's unconditional love.
it whispered to my heart, gifting solace to my soul.

my mind wandered
until the comforting touch of my wife's hand on my arm
snapped me back,
just as i had done for mum.

we prayed and bowed at my sister's grave
next to mum,
as the leaves in the nearby oak trees rustled,

finding solace in knowing my sister and mum
are eternally united.

in future visits to brookwood,
will i find comfort? only time will tell.
for now, this pain shows no signs of ceasing for me,

as my dear father would soon join mum,
laid together in eternal rest.

JANUARY 14TH

Let me come round
to your welcoming smile,
kiss your cheek,
hug and stay a while.

Today is January the 14th,
your special day;
let me light a candle,
make a wish and say,

"Happy Birthday, Mum!"

I remember how we would celebrate
and cut your cake.
Without you being here,
I'm staring at an empty plate.

Reality hits me hard
as I imagine the smile on your face,
candles flickering, music playing.
My heart plays a sad refrain.

The photographs we took
now help to ease the pain.
How I wish you hadn't gone.
How I pray that you had stayed.

I lift a glass to make a toast
to our wonderful past,
filled with more love and joy
than anyone could ever ask for.

Our time together,
I would never exchange.
I'd live each second
the very same way.

Every memory is a precious jewel,
which I'll hold tightly forever,
deep in my heart's treasury.
Until we embrace in Paradise,
each year you'll hear me vocalise:

"It is January the 14th today,
Mum's very special day."

PLEASE DON'T SAY

Please don't say,   "You'll never forget her."
She gave me life,
protected me.
I will never forget her.

Please don't say,   "I know how you feel."
Was she your mother, too?

Please don't say,   "Time is a healer."
Hers was a lifelong sacrifice.
My pain knows no time.

Please don't say,   "You'll remember the good times."
Every second was precious,
good or 'bad'.

Please don't say,   "It was her time to go."
Why was it? Who decides?
I should acquiesce; it was her time.

Please don't say, "Be strong."
She taught me to cry
if I felt sad or weak.

Please don't say, "Be strong for her."
She taught me to laugh
when I was happy.

Please don't say, "God wanted her to be with him."
She is still needed here!

Please don't say, "There is a reason for everything."
Or tell me what it is.

Please don't say, "She's in a better place."
Have you been there?
Do you know?

Please don't say, "She lived a long life."
I miss her
in this life.

FATHER AND SON

As hospital visiting ended, I stood to take my leave.
The air was heavily scented with disinfectant.
I noticed, from the corner of the room,
a frail, older man waving to me.

I was caught in a moment of indecision:
leave or remain?
But something tugged at my heart,
and I knew I couldn't just leave.

His fragility was evident as he rose
unsteadily to his feet. Bent and leaning
on his walking stick, he began to stagger
weakly towards me.

His discerning eyes locked with mine:
a connection so deep, I felt it in my spine.
Placing his trembling hand lightly on my shoulder,
he ushered me close, to say, soft and eloquently:

"I've been watching you, my dear boy,
for two months now, and have been absorbed by
how attentive you have been to your dear father.
The love and dedication you've shown your father
is admirable and a beautiful sight."

His words pierced through with such loving intent,
I could feel the depth of all he meant.

Pausing, he took a laboured breath.

"I pray, in times like these, my son will be awakened,
to care for me the way you have cared
with love and compassion,
and for me not to be forsaken."

Touched by his words,
I fought back my tears, and replied:

"If there is an option, sir,
I'm not aware of one,
nor do I wish to know,
for he is my dear father,
and I his only son."

THERE WILL NEVER BE ANOTHER

His arms were our shelter;
his hands, our providers.
His voice was filled with wisdom,
guiding each and every decision.
There will *never* be another.

A selflessly true gentleman,—
how richly blessed we were
to have had a father so wonderful.
He was truly like no other.

He had a warm smile matched by a caring heart.
He was endlessly giving, generous from the start.

Magnificent as a lion,
strong and brave,
through sacrifice and heartache,
he taught us oh so well.
There will *never* be another.

The journey you take now, Father,
you must take alone,
to be reunited with your wife
and your daughter upon a heavenly throne.

Until we meet again, you'll remain
engraved in our hearts,
for this is not a long farewell,
just some time apart.
Never, never will there be another.

ABOUT THE AUTHOR

Mem Ferda is a celebrated British actor, award-winning film producer and now poet, whose profound life journey resonates through every facet of his creativity. Born in South-West London to a Turkish diplomat father and a polyglot mother, he developed a passion for acting from a very young age. After achieving a BSc Psychology Honours degree and a Masters degree in business administration (MBA), he pursued acting training and graduated with a Postgraduate Degree in Classical Acting (PGDA) from the prestigious LAMDA (London Academy of Music and Dramatic Art). His enthusiasm to perfect his craft led to further classes and workshops at RADA (Royal Academy of Dramatic Art).

With over two hundred film and TV credits, he has starred alongside Hollywood heavyweights, often portraying heroic and villainous characters. His performances have seen him share the screen with Ray Liotta and Jason Statham in Guy Ritchie's *Revolver* (2005), Idris Elba in *Legacy* (2010), and Dominic Cooper in *The Devil's Double* (2011). In 2012, Mem starred as a lead in Nicolas Winding Refn's remake of the cult film, *Pusher*. He later appeared with Drew Barrymore and Toni Collette in *Miss You Already* (2015).

The constant demand from casting directors and global fans has kept Mem striving for more in acting and producing. He has often landed lead roles in genre films, which include *Hard Tide* (2015), *Smoking Guns* (2016), *Breakdown* (2016), *Eliminators* (2016) and *London Heist* (2017).

Mem is bilingual, speaking English and Turkish fluently, and he has a mastery of accents from Eastern European to American and native English accents. At 6 feet 2 inches, Mem captivates audiences with his rugged charisma and commanding presence. Drawing from a life as colourful as some of the characters he leaves burnt into our memories, Mem imbues his performances with pure authenticity. As a child, he witnessed an assassination attempt on his father. During his rebellious teens, he narrowly avoided being the getaway driver in a real-life heist! In Istanbul, he was threatened at gunpoint. Through sheer luck, he also cheated death from the *Marchioness* disaster of 1989.

Alongside his acting and producing career, Mem is a dedicated philanthropist and supports various international charities.

After a devastating accident in 2023, Mem unveiled his literary talent through the raw, cathartic poetry collection *HAPPYAGONY* – a selection of poems by Mem Ferda. Drawing from the dramatic highs and lows of his life's story, Mem's artistry now extends from the screen to the written word, connecting with fans worldwide through his uniquely powerful voice.